EXTREME

Survival!

Staying Alive in the Wild

Ross Piper

A & C Black • London

Produced for A & C Black by

MONKEY PUZZLE MEDIA LTD

Monkey Puzzle Media Ltd
The Rectory, Eyke, Woodbridge
Suffolk IP12 2QW, UK

Published by A & C Black Publishers Limited
38 Soho Square, London W1D 3HB

First published 2008
Copyright © 2008 A & C Black Publishers Limited

ISBN 978-1-4081-0014-1 (hardback)
ISBN 978-1-4081-0091-2 (paperback)

The right of Ross Piper to be identified as the
author of this Work has been asserted by him in
accordance with the Copyright, Designs and
Patents Act 1988.

A CIP catalogue record for this book is available
from the British Library.

Editor: Polly Goodman
Design: Mayer Media Ltd
Picture research: Lynda Lines
Series consultant: Jane Turner

This book is produced using paper that is made
from wood grown in managed, sustainable forests.
It is natural, renewable and recyclable. The logging
and manufacturing processes conform to the
environmental regulations of the country of origin.

Printed in China by C & C Offset Printing Co., Ltd

Picture acknowledgements
Alamy pp. 1 (Enigma), 10 (Niall Benvie), 11 inset
(Enigma); Corbis pp. 15 (Jayanta Shaw/Reuters), 17
inset (Envision), 20 (Eric and David Hosking), 21
(Robert van der Hilst), 27 (Jacqes Langevin/Sygma);
Empics p. 14 (AP); Flickr pp. 18, 28 both; FLPA p. 4
(Jan Vermeer/Foto Natura); Getty Images pp. 12
(National Geographic), ; iStockphoto p. 5 (Le Do);
Trevor Leat p. 16; MPM Images pp. 17, 22 both, 23
both, 29; Nature Picture Library p. 8 (Jim Clare);
Outdoorzy.com p. 19; Photolibrary.com pp. 7 (David
Messent), 9 (Graye Roessier/Index Stock Imagery),
13 (Himani Himani/Pacific Stock), 13 inset (Riou
Riou/Photocuisine), 26 (Bob Gibbons/OSF);
Picasaweb p. 6; Science Photo Library p. 11 (Adam
Hart-Davis); Texasbeyondhistory.net pp. 24, 25;
Wildrix.wordpress.com p. 25 inset.

The front cover shows a wilderness survival
instructor (Corbis/Bob Krist).

Every effort has been made to contact copyright
holders of material reproduced in this book. Any
omissions will be rectified in subsequent printings
if notice is given to the publishers.

CONTENTS

Abbreviations **m** stands for metres • **ft** stands for feet • **ml** stands for millilitres • **fl oz** stands for fluid ounces

Lifesavers

Imagine being lost in the middle of the vast Siberian plains, or deep in the Amazon rainforest. Would you know how to find food, water, or shelter? If not, read on!

Almost half of the world's surface is wilderness – places that humans rarely go. With no shelter, no food and no one around to help, getting lost in the wilderness is no joke. Fortunately, some things do survive in the wilderness – plants. If you know how to use them, plants can save your life.

Deadly berries

Lots of plants produce brightly coloured berries. Some of these are **edible**, but others are deadly poisonous. If you're not absolutely sure, leave them alone.

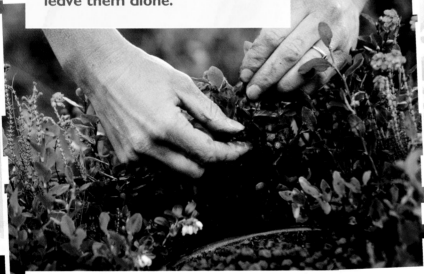

Blueberries contain lots of energy and are good survival food. They can be collected in the autumn.

rainforest an area of forest where there is lots of rain all year round

4

Many parts of the bamboo plant could help you survive in the wilderness.

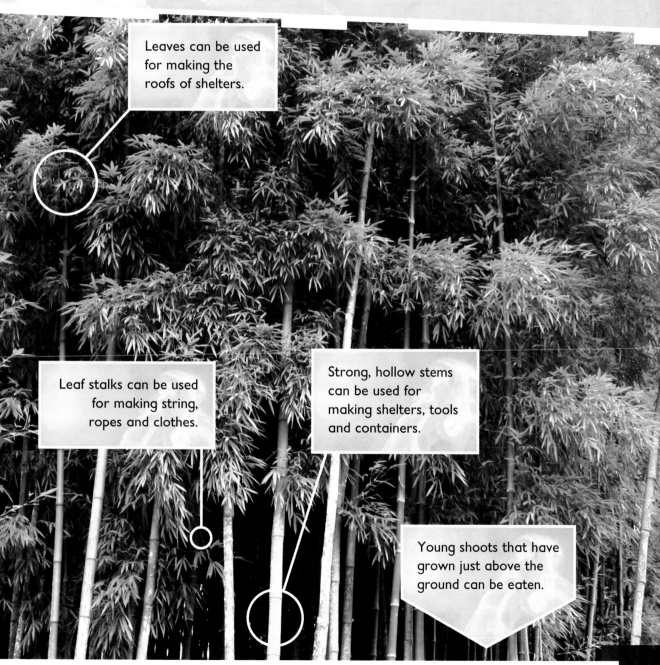

Leaves can be used for making the roofs of shelters.

Leaf stalks can be used for making string, ropes and clothes.

Strong, hollow stems can be used for making shelters, tools and containers.

Young shoots that have grown just above the ground can be eaten.

edible something that can be eaten

Tap in the trees

Dying of thirst in a tropical rainforest? There might be a river or stream nearby, but the water probably contains germs and parasites that could kill you. Try the water vine instead.

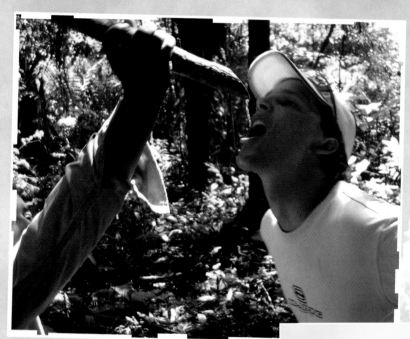

If the water vine is cut open, all the water it contains flows out of the cut.

The water vine is a woody plant that climbs other plants. It provides clean drinking water – like a tap in the trees! All plants transport water from their roots to their leaves, but the water vine is brilliant at transporting it under its woody bark. If you cut a piece of vine, a stream of clear, running water will flow out.

Medicine vines

The liquid in water vines is called **sap**. All plants have sap. Rainforest people use the sap in water vines as medicine.

parasites animals or plants that live and feed off others

Water flows through tiny tubes underneath the vine's bark.

The vine uses a tree as support, clinging to it and winding its way up to the **canopy**.

The roots are in the soil.

Water is sucked up from the roots to the leaves in the canopy.

canopy the top layer of a forest   **sap** a watery fluid that travels through plants carrying nutrients

Deadly sap

Some rainforest plants contain poison in their sap. The poison can be deadly, but if you know how to use it, it could stop you starving.

Rainforest trees have to protect themselves from the hungry mouths of plant-eating animals. The curare vine has poison called curare in its sap. Rainforest people dip the tips of darts into the poison. Then they use the darts in **blowpipes** to kill monkeys and birds for food.

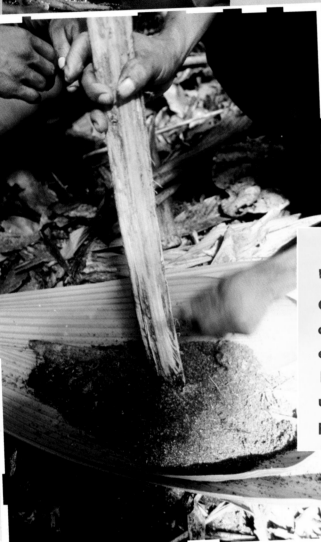

Just relax...

Curare can be deadly, but it can also be used to make operations easier. It was first used this way in 1942 by Dr Harold Griffith, who used it to relax the muscles of a patient he was operating on.

The curare plant is ground into a powder before it is mixed with water to make a sticky, poisonous goo.

blowpipes simple weapons used for firing darts

Dart shoots out towards prey.

The hunter blows hard into his pipe so the dart shoots out and hits his target.

Darts

Curare paste

Darts go in here.

A hunter in the Amazon rainforest, in Peru, dips his darts into curare poison before putting them in his blowpipe.

Fire starter

It's getting dark and cold. You need to make a fire, but what do you do if you have no lighter or matches?

*You can use a magnifying glass to focus the Sun's rays on some **tinder** and start a fire.*

If you're lost in the wilderness, knowing how to light a fire can be the difference between life and death. A fire keeps you warm, cooks your food, and keeps wild animals away from your camp. But remember, make sure your fire is completely out before you leave so you don't start a forest fire.

tinder   very dry plant material used for starting a fire

Drill turns in the notch on the fireboard. The **friction** produces heat until eventually, a tiny ember is produced.

The ember is carefully collected and surrounded by tinder, which is very dry and catches fire easily.

Blowing into the ball of tinder gives the fire oxygen and makes it grow.

A bow and drill is used to make a red-hot ember and start a fire. People have used this technique for thousands of years.

String of bow moves backwards and forwards, and turns the drill.

Fireboard

The bow is pushed back and forth like a saw.

friction the force of something rubbing against something else

Nuts about coconuts

Imagine being washed up on a small island, thousands of miles from anywhere, with coconut palms the only thing in sight. You're in luck – those trees are lifesavers.

A roof is thatched with coconut palm leaves.

Coconut palms are amazing – they provide food, clothing, shelter and medicine, too. All parts of the tree are useful, but especially the seeds, or coconuts. Like all seeds, coconuts are spread as far as possible and because they float, they can be carried away by waves. Coconuts can be a lifeline to desert-island castaways.

Root medicine

The roots of the coconut palm can be mashed in water to make a disinfectant mouthwash and medicine.

nutrients food substances that all living things need to survive

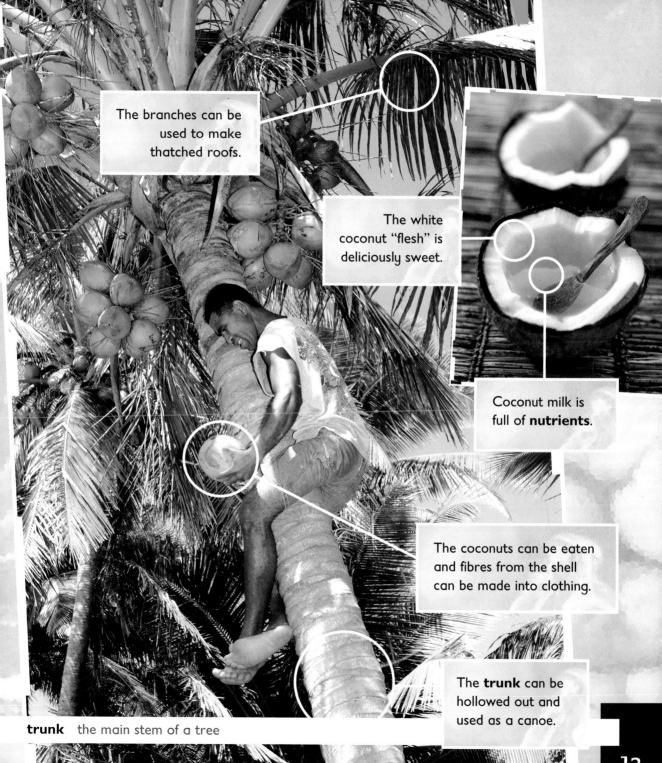

The branches can be used to make thatched roofs.

The white coconut "flesh" is deliciously sweet.

Coconut milk is full of **nutrients**.

The coconuts can be eaten and fibres from the shell can be made into clothing.

The **trunk** can be hollowed out and used as a canoe.

trunk the main stem of a tree

Coconut survivor!

In his own words

"Whenever I was hungry, I got a coconut and cut it. I drank the water, and ate the flesh. When it rained, I put my palms together and collected the water, and then drank it all."
– Michael Mangal describes how he survived.

Imagine being stranded for over three weeks, completely alone, not knowing if you are going to survive.

That is exactly what happened to a man called Michael Mangal, who lived on the Nicobar Islands in the Indian Ocean. On Boxing Day, 2004, these islands were in the direct path of a giant wave, a **tsunami**. Michael was washed out to sea and then dropped back on to land, only to find that everyone else on his island had been killed. He survived for 25 days by eating coconuts and drinking rainwater, before he was finally rescued.

Michael finally managed to attract a passing ship using a flag made from his underwear.

tsunami   a huge wave caused by an undersea earthquake

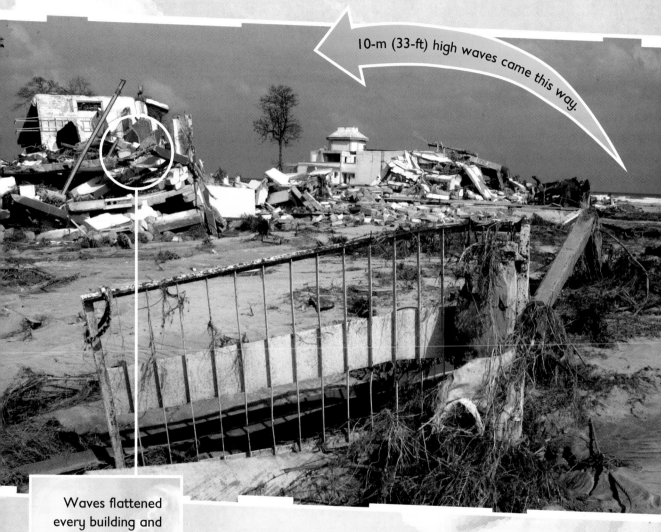

10-m (33-ft) high waves came this way.

Waves flattened every building and carried people back out to sea.

Flattened buildings on one of the Nicobar islands after the 2004 Boxing Day tsunami in the Indian Ocean.

Willow relief

If you catch a cold in the wilderness, the nearest doctor could be hundreds of miles away. But find a willow tree and it could take away your aches and pains!

Insects love to nibble the leaves of the willow tree, but too much nibbling will kill the tree. The willow stops these hungry mouths by producing a bitter-tasting chemical. The chemical is very similar to aspirin and it has been used as a painkiller since ancient times.

The springy branches of the willow tree can be woven into shelters, fencing and baskets. The bark is so bendy it can be used like string, to tie pieces of wood together.

A willow snack

You can eat some parts of the **Arctic** willow, a small tree that grows in the freezing Arctic. Peel the tender shoots on the branches and roots and eat the soft insides. A small handful of young Arctic willow leaves contains the same amount of **Vitamin C** as 7 to 10 oranges.

Arctic   the frozen area at and around the North Pole

Willow bark tea relieves aches and pains from colds and flu.

Aspirin pills contain the same painkilling chemicals as are found in willow bark.

1. Peel off a bit of bark from the thin branches of a willow tree and dunk it in a cup of boiling water. All parts of the willow tree contain a chemical similar to aspirin, but the bark contains the most.

2. Chemicals in the bark seep into the water.

Vitamin C one of 13 different vitamins that humans need to stay healthy

Super shelters

You're lost in some woods without a tent and it's starting to get dark. Fortunately, you're probably surrounded by trees that could keep you alive.

Knowing how to build a shelter in the wilderness can be a lifesaver. Wherever you are in the world, there are trees that are suitable for building shelters. A tree with strong, flexible branches is perfect. Using these branches and some leaves you can make excellent shelters that will keep you warm, dry and protect you from biting insects.

This shelter is made from a frame of sticks covered by leaves. It's excellent for cold places because the leaves trap heat inside.

Picking the spot

A shelter built in a carefully chosen place will be the most comfortable. Woods will protect you from the worst of the wind and the rain. Avoid low-lying areas and dips because your shelter could be flooded if it rains.

crossbar a horizontal stick or bar

This simple shelter, made from the branches of a sycamore tree, is perfect for when it's not too cold.

1. Stick two uprights (straight sticks with forked ends) into the ground.

2. Rest a **crossbar** stick in the forks of the uprights.

3. Add diagonal support sticks to the uprights and tie together with string.

4. Rest branches with lots of leaves along the crossbar.

Position shelter towards the fire for warmth.

Dry grass and dead leaves make a soft bed.

Rocks provide added support to the uprights.

19

Bulging baobabs

Juicy fruits

Baobab fruits contain six times more Vitamin C than oranges. The fruit juice makes a drink a bit like lemonade. It is also used to treat fevers by tribes in Southern Africa.

In Southern Africa, temperatures can reach a scorching 50 degrees Centigrade (122 degrees Fahrenheit) and there's very little rain. Here, the baobab, one of the oddest-looking trees on the planet, is essential for survival.

Desert plants survive by storing water and this is what the baobab is best at. Its fat, hollow trunk can hold up to 120,000 litres (26,350 gallons) of water. Find a baobab and you can quench your thirst. You can also take shade from the hot sun in its huge, hollow trunk.

Two halves of a baobab fruit.

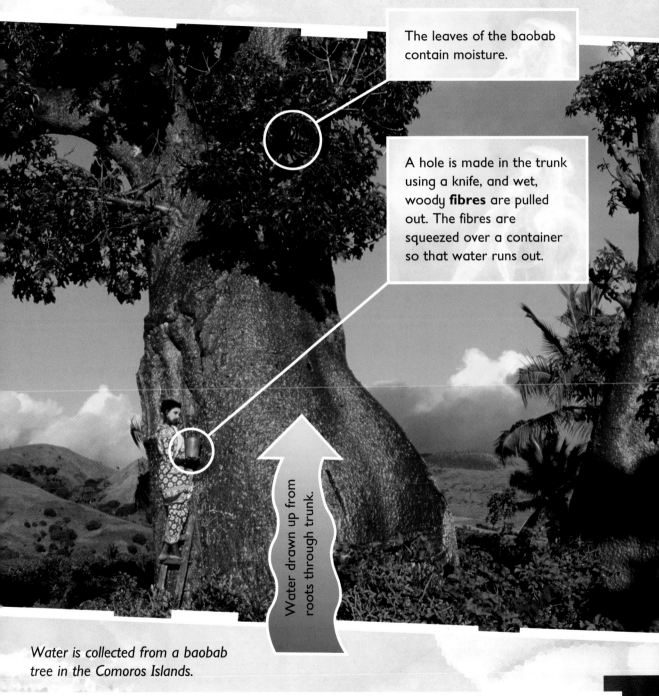

The leaves of the baobab contain moisture.

A hole is made in the trunk using a knife, and wet, woody **fibres** are pulled out. The fibres are squeezed over a container so that water runs out.

Water drawn up from roots through trunk.

Water is collected from a baobab tree in the Comoros Islands.

fibres   the stringy threads that make up most plants

Water traps

Run out of water? Surrounded by plants? Then you're safe. All you need is a clear plastic bag and a piece of string.

One easy way to get water, wherever you are, is by trapping the water produced by plants. Water constantly travels up through plants from their roots and **evaporates** from their leaves during the day. You can trap this water using a plastic bag.

Every part of the yew tree is poisonous to humans.

Poisonous water

Be careful what tree you choose to collect water from because some, like the yew, produce poisonous sap that could contaminate the water and make you ill!

evaporates   turns from a liquid into a gas

1. Put a plastic bag over a branch with lots of leaves and tie the bag in place with some string. Leave in the sunshine for about 4 hours.

2. Water vapour from leaves **condenses** into water droplets.

Water travels to leaves from roots.

Water evaporates

Water evaporates

Water evaporates

Water evaporates

4. Return to the bag and tip the water into a cup or glass. You can collect 250 ml (9 fl oz) of water in 4 hours using this simple technique.

3. Water droplets collect at bottom of bag.

condenses turns from a gas into a liquid

Back to the roots

You will need to brave cold water and gooey mud to get at the useful bits of the bulrush. But in a watery wasteland, it could keep you alive!

Plants make food using sunlight, water and carbon dioxide. Some plants store this food underground to help them survive the winter. The bulrush plant stores its food in its swollen roots. These are a **nutritious** and energy-rich snack.

A bulrush plant is pulled up from the edge of a pond in the USA. Almost every part of the bulrush plant was used by Native Americans.

Bulrush salad

The young leaves of the bulrush can be cooked or eaten raw in a salad.

nutritious   containing lots of nutrients, substances that all living things need to survive

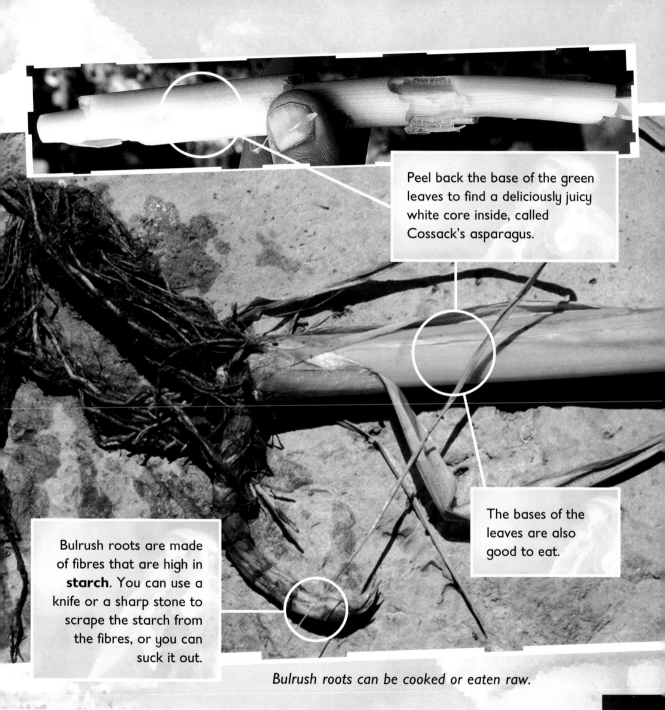

Peel back the base of the green leaves to find a deliciously juicy white core inside, called Cossack's asparagus.

The bases of the leaves are also good to eat.

Bulrush roots are made of fibres that are high in **starch**. You can use a knife or a sharp stone to scrape the starch from the fibres, or you can suck it out.

Bulrush roots can be cooked or eaten raw.

starch a food substance that is high in energy and very easy to digest

Siberian survival

Siberia is no place to get lost without warm clothes, but over 80 years ago hundreds of Russian prisoners braved this immense wilderness to reach freedom.

Between the 1920s and the 1950s, millions of Russians were held in very harsh prison camps in Siberia. Those who escaped had to walk hundreds of kilometres across freezing, empty wastes. They put the fluffy seeds of bulrushes in the lining of their coats and trousers to stop them freezing to death. The seeds added a layer of **insulation**, which trapped body heat.

Bulrush flowers releasing their fluffy seeds. This fluff kept escapees from Russian prison camps warm for the many weeks it took them to reach freedom and safety.

insulation   anything that prevents the loss of warmth by trapping air

Hundreds of kilometres to the nearest town.

Prisoners lived in these cold, simple buildings. They were forced to work long hours in mines, where they dug for gold, diamonds and dangerous metals.

Temperatures in the long, cold winters dropped to -71°C (-96°F).

These buildings are all that remain of a prison camp in northern Siberia, north of the Arctic Circle.

Escape to freedom

In 1942, seven prisoners escaped from a Siberian prison camp and walked 6,400 kilometres (4,000 miles) through the most inhospitable wilderness on Earth. They ate anything they could find, including snakes, and their incredible journey took 11 months. Four of the men died along the way, but the survivors eventually reached India and freedom.

Survival kit

We can survive in some surprising places if we know how. Remember, almost anywhere that plants can survive, we can probably survive too.

There are thousands of different plants that can make the difference between life and death. Learn all you can about them, because you never know when it may come in handy. If you're heading out on a long hike, pack a simple survival kit like the one opposite to help in case you get lost.

A flint bar is struck against a striking blade to produce sparks and start a fire.

Penknife including a saw blade: useful for cutting branches, hunting and cooking.

Small cooking tin: for holding food, water and the rest of the survival kit.

Compass: to help find your way.

Flint bar and striking blade: for making a fire.

Tough string: for making traps and securing shelters.

Safety pins: very useful for holding things together.

Fishing hooks: for catching fish.

Survival blanket: keeps you warm in an emergency.

Needle and strong thread: for mending clothes and other fabric items such as tents.

Glossary

Arctic the frozen area at and around the North Pole

blowpipes simple weapons used for firing darts

canopy the top layer of a forest

condenses turns from a gas into a liquid

crossbar a horizontal stick or bar

edible something that can be eaten

evaporates turns from a liquid into a gas

fibres the stringy threads that make up most plants

friction the force of something rubbing against something else

insulation anything that prevents the loss of warmth by trapping air

nutrients food substances that all living things need to survive

nutritious containing lots of nutrients, food substances that all living things need to survive

parasites animals or plants that live and feed off others

rainforest an area of forest where there is lots of rain all year round

sap a watery fluid that travels through plants carrying nutrients

starch a food substance that is high in energy and very easy to digest

tinder very dry plant material used for starting a fire

trunk the main stem of a tree

tsunami a huge wave caused by an undersea earthquake

Vitamin C one of 13 different vitamins that humans need to stay healthy

Further information

Books

Bushcraft Skills and How to Survive in the Wild: A Step-by-Step Practical Guide by Anthonio Akkermans (Southwater Books, 2007)
Gives a simple step-by-step guide to surviving in the wild, with lots of pictures.

Essential Bushcraft by Ray Mears (Hodder & Stoughton, 2003)
Lots of photographs that show you how to build shelters, find food and survive.

Science of Survival: The Ultimate Survival Guide for Boys by Mike Flynn (Macmillan Children's Books, 2008)
Learn how to plot a map, navigate using the stars, and other survival skills.

Survival by Chris Ryan (Red Fox, 2002)
An action-packed thriller about five kids marooned on a desert island and what they do to survive.

Wild Food by Ray Mears (Hodder & Stoughton, 2007)
This book shows you how to get food, especially edible plants, in the wild, which will help you survive in harsh conditions.

Television

Ray Mears' Extreme Survival series (Day Gardner Productions, 2003)
Two series of programmes showing how to survive in extreme places.

Ray Mears – Bushcraft Survival (Woodlore, 2005)
Two series of programmes with lots of bushcraft tips, including how to build shelters and find food.

Tribe (BBC, 2007)
Three series of programmes giving lots of information on how tribes around the world survive using skills and traditions passed down over thousands of years.

Websites

www.primitiveways. com/
This detailed website shows you how to make things that enable you to survive in the wilderness. All the techniques are based on the ancient skills used by tribes people around the world.

www.pfaf.org/
This website provides a massive list of useful plants and what they can be used for, including building, food and medicine.

http://wildwoodsurvival. com/
Lots of brilliant tips for surviving in the wild.

http://dsc.discovery.com/ convergence/survival/ guide/guide.html
The Discovery Channel Survival Zone website, including lots of information on extreme situations and how humans survive in them.

Index